Don't Mess with Moses!

Don't Mess with Moses!

peculiar poems
and rib-tickling rhymes

Marty Nystrom

illustrated by Steve Björkman

Standard® PUBLISHING
Bringing The Word to Life

Cincinnati, Ohio

Project editor: Laura Derico
Cover design: John Hamilton/The Design Works Group, Inc.
Interior design: Robin Black/The Design Works Group, Inc.
Illustrator photo: Carl Björkman

ISBN 0-7847-1833-4

12 11 10 09 08 07 06   9 8 7 6 5 4 3 2 1

Library of Congress Cataloging-in-Publication Data
Nystrom, Marty.
    Don't mess with Moses! : peculiar poems and rib-tickling rhymes / Marty Nystrom ; illustrated by Steve Björkman.
        p. cm.
    Includes index.
    ISBN 0-7847-1833-4 (casebound)
  1. Bible--Juvenile poetry. 2. Children's poetry, American. 3. Humorous poetry, American.
I. Title.
PS3614.Y7D66 2006
811'.6--dc22

                                                    2005035376

To my father, Donald H. Nystrom,
who taught me to enjoy rhyme, be refreshed by laughter,
and above all love God and his Word.
MARTY

For Riley, Ford, and Brady Goodfellow.
STEVE

Contents

Introduction 8

True Tales 10

Eternal God 12

The Good Book 14

More Than HE-roes 15

The Very First Week 16

Light 18

Sky 19

Finger Lickin' Good 20

Creepy Crawlies 21

Grand Imagination 22

Grandpa Is Not a Gorilla 24

Easy Pickin's 26

Adam's Family 28

Deprived 29

Messy 30

Sideache 32

First Love 33

Dalmatian Dot 34

Just Say NO! 36

Cain and Abel 37

Towering Inferno 38

High-Waters 39

Noah, Noah 40

Animal Collector 42

No One Notices 43

Love Boat 44

Snail's Pace 46

Skunks 48

Incognito 49

Water, Water, Everywhere 50

Shhhhhh! 52

Antsy 54

Praying Mantis 55

All You Can Eat 56

Baby Boom 57

Camel Complaint 58

Flying Colors 60

A Little Rain 62

Stairway to the Stars 63

Misunderstanding 64

Salt Block 66

Abraham 67

Star Search 68

No Kiddin' 70

Where Are We Goin'? 72

Rebekah's Trek 74

Birthright Broth 75

Jacob's Lament 76

Wrestling Match 78

Joseph's Fashion Show 80

Confession 81

Dreamer 82

Family Reunion 83

Baby Moses 84

Speechless 86

Countdown 88

Invasion of the Swamp Creatures 92

Small Problem 94

Just a Few Things 95

Old Man and the Sea 96

Don't Mess with Moses! 98

A New Song and Dance 100
Manna 102
Rock Springs 104
God Rules 105
Golden Calves 106
Laying Down the Law 108
Fault Line 110
Why?-ners 112
Donkey Talk 114
Fightin' Chants 115
Wall of Sound 116
Time Warp 118
A Woman's Place 119
Jael 120
Boondoggled 121
Tough Love 122
Pumping Iron 124
Hair-Razing Tale 125
In-Law Lessons 126
Sleepyhead 128
Old King Saul 130
Hotshot 131
Fit for a King 132
Giant Size 134
Saul's Armor 136
Dog Fight 138
Last Words 140
Friends 142
Dancin' Dave 144
Absalom 146

David's Diary 148
The Lord Is My Shepherd 149
Thirsty Deer 150
Heart Praise 152
Wonderfully Made 154
Whiz Kid 156
Split Decision 158
Writer's Cramp 159
Rain Man 160
Raven-ous 161
Showdown 162
Don't You Be Like Jezebel 164
Speedy King Jehu 165
King Rehoboam 166
Battle Hymn 168
A Royal Pain 170
Queen Esther's Quest 171
Lean Green Cuisine 172
Shadrach, Meshach,
   and Abednego 174
Fourth Man 176
Miracles 177
Finicky Felines 178
Purrfect Pillow 180
Bones 182
Bellyache 184
Bible Names 186
Flaws 187
Multiple Choice 188
Indexes 190

Introduction

The Bible is anything but boring! Its pages are filled with some of history's most colorful characters and exciting events. Many of these Bible situations are downright hilarious when seen with a sense of humor.

I smile when I think about those folks who believed they could build a tower all the way to the stars. I love to imagine the startled expression on Balaam's face when his donkey began to talk to him. And think of all the funny things that are likely to happen when oodles of animals are gathered together on one big boat!

Along with the humor, the Bible is jam-packed with stories that help us learn important things about our own lives. I hope these poems make you chuckle, make you think, and make you curious to look into God's Word to find out more. Enjoy!

My heartfelt gratitude goes out to all who helped me, including my Thursday morning writing group: Judy Bodmer, Thorn Ford, Peg Kehle, Kate Lloyd, Paul Malm, and Laurie Winslow Sargent. Thank you for your prayer support and your loving and constructive encouragement.

Thank you to those who have been a creative influence in my life and have provided open doors for me to express my gifts—in particular, Michael Coleman, Don Moen, Dr. Carl and Karen Berner, Pastors Jim and Betsey Hayford, Laura Derico, and Standard Publishing.

Thanks also to my parents, Don and Elajean Nystrom, and my seven siblings, who have provided decades of laughter and love; to my sons, Nathan and Benjamin, whose humor and personalities are woven through these pages; and to my wife, Jeanne, so full of life, who lovingly and graciously remains supportive of her right-brained husband.

True Tales

There's a soul-stirring book
     full of spine-tingling tales
  of villains and heroes
and man-eating whales;

of princes and pharaohs,
  of masters and slaves,
    of kings hunting outlaws
      that hide out in caves;

      of prophets and preachers,
     of scholars and teachers,
    of merchants and shepherds,
   and all kinds of creatures,

        like talkative donkeys
         and bloodthirsty cats,
          kindhearted ravens
          and huge clouds of gnats;

        of tall man-made towers
        and creature-filled boats,
        of tyrants and giants
        and colorful coats;

TRUST ME!

of soldiers and cowards,
of slippery spies,
of wise men and fools,
and snakes that tell lies;

of trillions of frogs
that take over the town,
of mighty stone walls
that come tumbling down;

of fantastic visions
and fanciful dreams,
of lousy decisions
and devilish schemes;

of heartwarming stories
and words of advice,
with serious lessons
on how to live life.

These tales are not fables
from out of the blue;
these tales in the Bible
are totally true!

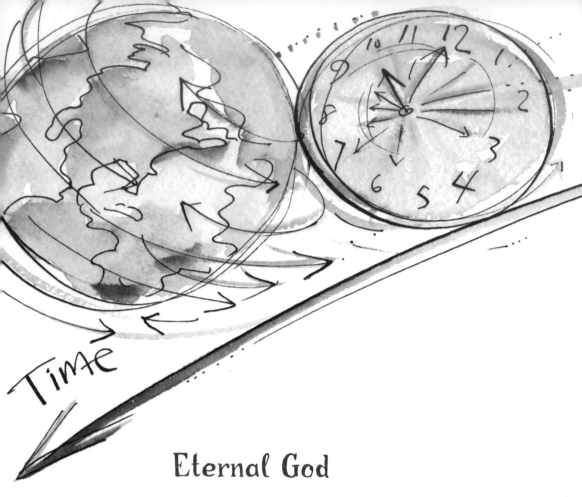

Time

Eternal God

God had no beginning,
    and God will have no end—
        now there's a tricky concept
            for a kid to comprehend.

The Good Book

The stories in the Bible
are so stunning and stellar,
it's no wonder why
God's Word is still
the world's best seller.

14

More Than HE-roes

The Bible has a whole lot of heroes
like Abraham and Moses,
Joshua and Joseph,
Gideon and Job, to name a few;
the Bible also has a lot of SHE-roes—
it tells of many mighty women too.

Deborah was a wise and trusted leader,
Jael bravely nailed the enemy,
Ruth was always faithful and courageous,
and Esther's boldness set her people free.

By looking at the list above,
it's clear as clear can be—
the Lord will use us just as much
be we a he or she.

The Very First Week

On Monday God created light
to separate the day from night.

On Tuesday he made the big blue sky;
he stretched it wide and he made it high.

On Wednesday he formed the land and seas,
the mountains and valleys, the flowers and trees.

On Thursday all the stars were spun,
the comets and planets, the moon and the sun.

On Friday he filled the sea and the sky
with creatures that swim and creatures that fly.

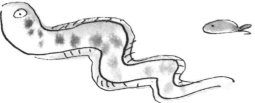

On Saturday he built every beast
that lives upon the land,

and finally last, but surely not least,
God created man.

On Sunday God looked on the world
and said that it was good;
he then enjoyed a day of rest
in his brand-new neighborhood.

Read about God's amazing week in Genesis 1:1–2:4.

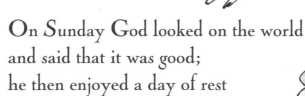

Light

I'm glad the Lord invented light
so we could tell the day from night,
for I am such a sleepyhead,
you bet I'd forget
when to roll out of bed.

"Then God said, 'Let there be light.'"
Read about it in Genesis 1:3-5.

Sky

What would we do
    without a sky?
Where would the jets
    and the eagles fly?
Where would we look
    on the Fourth of July
    to watch as rockets
    go whizzing by?
There'd be no sunsets
    to please the eye,
    and my brand-new kite
    wouldn't get very high.

You'll never catch me
    wonderin' why
God needed to make
the big blue sky.

God created the sky on the second day.
Read about it in Genesis 1:6-8.

Finger Lickin' Good

On day number five
God made alive
all kinds of birds and fishes,
so Mom could make,
and I could partake,
of all my favorite dishes:

Like
shrimp chow mein,
chicken strips,
and seafood fettuccini,
scrambled eggs,
fish and chips,
and turkey tetrazzini.

**"So God created great sea creatures and every sort
of fish and every kind of bird. And God saw that
it was good." Genesis 1:21**

Creepy Crawlies

Spooky spiders and big black beetles,
   scaly snakes and slimy slugs,
     awful ants and monster mosquitoes,
      wiggly worms and big brown bugs,

     loathsome lizards and repulsive rats,
      gross grasshoppers and buzzing bees,
       frightening frogs and nasty gnats—
        why did the Lord have to make all these?

    From all these creepy crawly things
    I wish the Lord would spare us
      'cause irritating boys at school
      use 'em just to scare us.

Grand Imagination

God has a grand imagination,
his ideas are enough to blow your mind.
Just look at all the critters in creation
that are absolutely one of a kind.

There's a pachyderm with a hose for a nose
and a shark with a hammer for his head;
there's a bright little fly that glows in the dark
and a rodent that pretends he is dead.

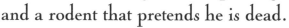

There's a lizard that changes his color
and a catfish that can actually walk;
there's an animal that wears plated armor
and an eel that delivers quite a shock!

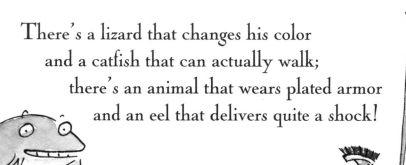

There are thousands of strange-looking beetles
and a feline as fast as a car;
there's a creature that's covered with needles
and a fish that is shaped like a star.

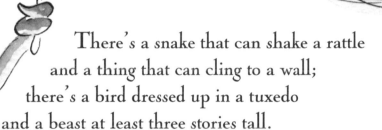

There's a snake that can shake a rattle
and a thing that can cling to a wall;
there's a bird dressed up in a tuxedo
and a beast at least three stories tall.

Now in case I haven't quite convinced you
of our God's awesome creativity,
just go and take a look in the mirror,
then tell me what kind of creature you see!

Grandpa Is Not a Gorilla

My grandpa is not a gorilla,
my sis doesn't swing in the trees,
my mom doesn't mimic a monkey,
and Dad doesn't forage for fleas.

My grandma is hardly a gibbon,
my aunt doesn't scratch her armpits,
my brother will not eat bananas,
unless they're in sundaes or splits.

My nephew can't walk on his knuckles,
my niece has no hair on her knees,
and none of my cousins or uncles
smell anything like chimpanzees.

So you can imagine the look on my face—
I sat with my mouth all agape—
while Teacher tried hard to convince me
I'm related to some kind of ape.

I know that my kinfolk aren't perfect—
we have chumps in our family tree—
but none of the gang's an orangutan,
so you can't make a monkey out of me!

**"So God created people in his own image;
God patterned them after himself." Genesis 1:27**

Easy Pickin's

Apples and oranges,
juicy and sweet,
plums and peaches—
all you can eat.
Everything's free,
for God is treatin';
I see why it's called
the Garden of Eatin'.

**Read about the garden in
Genesis 2:8-17.**

27

Adam's Family

I'm listed in the
Genesis Book of Records
for having the
shortest family tree.
Only two folks are included—
God and me.

Find out how God made Adam in Genesis 2:7.

Deprived

Adam had no cousins,
Adam had no toys,
he never went to recess,
or played ball with other boys.
Adam had no grandma
to tell him to be good,
'cause Adam never had
a childhood.

—No fair!

?

Messy

My mama says that I'm a mess,
 but surely it can't hurt
  to get some frosting on my face
   while eating my dessert.

And why does she get petty,
 and become so cross and curt,
  just because I spill spaghetti
   on her "dry clean only" skirt?

And does it really matter
    that I sometimes over-squirt
      and end up shooting ketchup
        on my brother's brand-new shirt?

        Good thing ol' Adam had no mom;
      he'd get his feelings hurt,
 'cause the Bible says that Adam was
completely made of dirt!

... Just bein'
biblical, Mom.

**Read about this in
Genesis 2:7.**

Sideache

Last week I learned in Sunday school
how God made Adam's bride.
He built her from a spare rib
that he took from Adam's side.

Today while playing soccer
I got the scare of my life:
my side was aching—
I thought God was making
my rib into a wife!

Did God really do that?
Read about it in Genesis 2:21-24.

First Love

When Eve met Adam
it was love at first sight.
(But then again,
who else could be
Mr. Right?!)

Dalmatian Dot

We have a dog.
We call her Dot
'cause she's a spotted Dalmatian.
Her name did not
require a lot
of our imagination.

But when she had eleven pups
early in the fall,
it took a lot
of extra thought
just to name 'em all.

There's
Leopard and Ladybug,
the slow one is Pokey;
Freckles and Fireplug,
the smallest is Smokey.

There's
Patches and Chicken Pox,
Cheetah and Ocelot,
and 'course it was natural
for there to be Spot.

It took a long time
to name this big litter
soon after our dog gave birth;
so think of poor Adam
who named EVERY critter
that lived on the face of the earth!

**Check out what Adam did
in Genesis 2:18-20.**

You think YOU'VE got a hard job to do?

Just Say NO!

Adam and Eve made a big mistake
and listened to the lies of a slippery snake.
They foolishly followed his false advice—
now everyone wishes
that they woulda thought twice!

So if a serpent comes aslitherin' along
and tries to convince you to do somethin' wrong,
remember what occurred
to that pair long ago:
learn from their lesson and just say
NO!

See this sad story in Genesis 3.

36

Cain and Abel

The very first brothers
that ever were
in human history
began the tradition
of that wretched condition
called sibling rivalry.

Cain and Abel's story is in Genesis 4.

Towering Inferno

Old, old man Methuselah,
how long did it actually take
to blow out all those candles
on your big ol' birthday cake?

**Just how old did Methuselah get?
See Genesis 5:27.**

38

High~Waters

Noah had three children:
Japheth, Ham, and Shem.
The kids at school were terribly cruel
and liked to make fun of them.

Those poor little boys of Noah's
never stood a chance,
'cause it wasn't cool to come to school
wearing high-water pants.

The other children taunted them
and started slinging mud,
"You wear your pants hiked up too high—
are you waitin' for a flood?!"

**Did Noah's sons know
something the other
kids didn't know?**

Noah, Noah

Noah, Noah, don't ya know a
plan so grand will never work?
Your silly scheme
is just a dream—
we think you've gone berserk!

Noah, Noah, don't ya know a
barge so large will never float?
Our desert town
is dry and brown—
    who needs a big ol' boat?

    Noah, Noah, don't ya know a
    rig so big will never sail?
    This hunk of junk's
    already sunk—
        this thing is
        bound to fail.

Hey
Dork!

Dummy!

Silly!

40

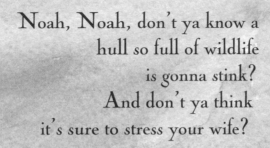

Noah, Noah, don't ya know a
hull so full of wildlife
is gonna stink?
And don't ya think
it's sure to stress your wife?

Noah, Noah, don't ya know your
claim to fame will only be
you built a yacht
on some big lot
that isn't near the sea?

Noah, Noah, don't ya know a—
drip, drip, drop—hey,
say, what was that?
It wasn't s'posed to rain today.
I'm going home to get my hat!

**Read about Noah in
Genesis 6:9-22.**

rain?

Animal Collector

Noah brought two boas from the jungle.
Noah got two goas from Tibet.
Noah sought jerboas in the desert
and caught a couple moas in a net.
But how did poor ol' Noah
find a pair of protozoa?
For the microscope
was not invented yet.

**What animals did God tell Noah to get?
See Genesis 7:1-3.**

No One Notices

No one notices Noah,
he gets no respect.
No one seems to
know that he's
a noted ark-itect.

Love Boat

The guests are beginning to gather,
arriving now in twos—
husbands and wives together,
to take an exclusive cruise.

Buck and Doeris Deer are here.
There's Billy and Nanny Goat.
Sowphie and Boaris Hogg appear
to take their places on the boat.

Henny and Tommy Turkey
and Ewenice and Ramsey Sheep
are busily checking the passenger list
to find out where they'll sleep.

There goes Jenny Mule
and her stubborn hubby, Jack,
packing Jenny's luggage
on his poor ol' aching back.

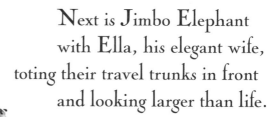

Next is Jimbo Elephant
with Ella, his elegant wife,
toting their travel trunks in front
and looking larger than life.

Here comes the regal King of Beasts
  with the queen of the lion pride.
    There's Mr. Giraffe and his better half,
    walking side by side.

    And taking their place in the long, long line
are Mr. and Mrs. Porcupine;
pinned to her back is a Just Married sign,
cut in the shape of a valentine.

     And coming this way is Mr. Peacock—
      so proud of his pretty peahen—
       strutting his stuff to the end of the dock,
       showing off his feathers again.

There's Whinny and Ed, the thoroughbreds,
  acting so crazy in love.
   That twosome looking like newlyweds
   is Mr. and Mrs. Dove.

    So on and on the animals come,
     and two by two they board
     to take their place on Noah's ark
     as honored guests of the Lord.

Snail's Pace

Make it snappy, little snails—
it's beginning to pour.
Make it snappy, little snails—
we've got to shut the door.
Make it snappy, little snails—
things are getting damp.
Make it snappy, little snails—
hurry up the ramp!

Step on it.

Skunks

Ain't this neat!
What a treat!
Noah gave us
a private suite.

Incognito

I think it's best we stay disguised—
that way we won't be recognized.
And we'll be in a good position
if Noah decides to do some fishin'.

Water, Water, Everywhere

Water, water, everywhere,
perfect for a polar bear.
Surely Noah wouldn't care
if I took a dip?

Water, water, everywhere,
tempting to a polar bear
when there's so much time to spare
on this lengthy trip.

Water, water, everywhere,
thrilling for a polar bear—
as I'm flying in mid-air,
I'll try my triple flip.

Water, water, everywhere,
not a speck of land out there.
Should I risk it, do I dare . . . ?

Naw . . . I better stay aboard the ship.

Shhhhhh!

All this babble is driving me batty.
How's a guy to get a good day's sleep?
Must you be so boisterous and chatty,
and moo and grunt and honk
and buzz and cheep?

I was designed to doze in the day,
'cause I'm up all hours of the night.
I can't help that I was made this way,
so please, won't you be polite?

52

You're loud enough to wake the dead
with all your noisy din,
and just about my time for bed
is when you all chime in.

So kindly hold back
all your yakety-yak;
remember the hours I keep.
It's time for me
to hit the sack,
and I don't want to hear a peep!

Antsy

"We better beware,"
said Mr. Ant
to his eensy-weensy wife.
"We must steer clear
of the anteater, dear,
if we hope to have a life."

"When you see that critter coming,
just run for all you're worth.
If we're consumed,
all antkind is doomed—
we're the last two ants on earth!"

Praying Mantis

Here I am on this great big boat,
on my very first overseas cruise.
Though my husband and I really needed a break,
this is not the type of trip that I would choose.

You see, I have an awful fear of water—
I never took the time to learn to swim.
I'm so scared when this ark begins to totter,
and my chances for survival seem slim.

But then I recall
that God is in control,
though everything around me looks grim.
I offer up a prayer,
giving God my every care,
knowing well that I can trust in him.

**"Commit everything you do to the Lord.
Trust him, and he will help you." Psalm 37:5**

All You Can Eat

The termites never missed a meal—
they had it pretty good.
Their situation was ideal—
the ark was made of wood!

**What kind of wood did Noah use?
See Genesis 6:14.**

Baby Boom

Something strange is happ'nin' here,
something sort o' funny—
I thought the only hares on board
were **Mr.** and **Mrs.** Bunny.

Camel Complaint

"Rain, rain, go away,"
cried Camille on the fortieth day.
"How much longer will it pour?
I just can't take it anymore!"

"I know that it's a blessing
to be sailing on this cruise,
but the weather's so depressing,
and I'm battling the blues."

"I don't mean to make a fuss,
to murmur and complain,
but we camels aren't accustomed
to a climate with much rain."

"I'm really not a grump,
it's just that my hump
is drowning in this ever-drenching drizzle.
I sound like a scrooge,
but this daily deluge
is causing all my fur to frizzle."

"The gator and the otter
are at home in all this water:
'The wetter, the better,' they say.
But all this pitter-patter
makes my teeth just clink and clatter
as I shiver in wet weather through the day."

"Surely you can understand,
I'm homesick for the desert sand,
and I cannot contain my sorrow.
I can only hope and pray
for an end to all this gray,
and that the sun will finally come
tomorrow."

**How many more days did poor
Camille have to wait? See Genesis 7.**

Flying Colors

When the flood was finally over
and all the earth was dry,
God made a brilliant banner,
and he flew it in the sky.

An iridescent crescent,
with a stylish striped design
of colors more fluorescent
than a giant neon sign.

Brushed with streaks of purple,
and with bands of blue and green,
with ribbons red and yellow
mixed with strands of tangerine.

Just like a bunch of bright balloons,
and like a rooster's tail,
or like a brand-new box of crayons
that Grandma sends by mail.

God stretched this streamer in the sky,
up high where I could see,
so I could be reminded
of his promises to me.

Read about God's promise in Genesis 9:8-17.

A Little Rain

They say that into every life
a little rain must fall,
that everything won't always go my way.
So I will not complain
when I see it start to rain.
(I'm just glad I didn't live in Noah's day.)

Stairway to the Stars

Long, long ago in a faraway land,
some people had a plan
to build a tower to the stars.
"We'll make it taller than the mountains," they boasted.
"We'll take it higher than the clouds," they bragged.
    "It'll reach beyond the moon,
    much farther than Neptune,
    past Jupiter and Saturn and Mars."
    But things didn't go as they expected,
    and construction came ascreechin' to a stop.
    The monument was suddenly neglected;
    the project was a first-rate flop.

    But if their plans had not been interrupted,
    those fools would still be building there today,
    'cause Alpha Centauri, our nearest star,
    is trillions of miles away.

How about
an elevator?

**Find out what went wrong for
these foolish builders
in Genesis 11:1-9.**

Misunderstanding

"Hey there, Hiram,
hand me the hammer!"
Clem called out
above the clamor.
Hiram only shook his head;
he had no clue
what Clem had said.

Hiram shouted,
"Meetaw boke."
(That's "No understand"
in the language he spoke.)

Clem called back,
"Hey, what'd ya say?
Tryin' to be a wise guy, eh?"

But "Blah, blah, blah"
was all Hiram heard;
he couldn't make sense
of a single word.

He yelled at Clem,
"Goo tee na bibberish!"

(Translated means,
"You're speaking gibberish!")

Clem cried out,
"Don't yammer and stammer.
Can't you speak with proper grammar?
Stop yer jabberin'
and hand me
that hammer!"

By now poor Hiram
had had enough—
he picked up his tools and left in a huff,
shouting at Clem,
"Nah bay doh wuff!"
("I don't need any more of your guff!")

All over the Babel project site
were spats and squabbles and feuds
and fights.
And so I guess
it's needless to say
that not much work
got done that day!

Salt Block

She had lots of warning,
so it was her own fault
that ol' Mrs. Lot
looked around and got
turned into a pile of salt.

Find out why this happened in Genesis 19:15-26.

Abraham

God promised Abraham
that he would be
the father of the
world's biggest family—
with billions of children
and grandbabies galore,
with scads of great-grandkids
that add up to more
than the stars in the sky
or the sands on the shore.

I guess you could say
from the size of his clan
that Abe was the ultimate
family man.

**Read about God's promise to Abraham
in Genesis 22:15-18.**

Star Search

Last night my brother Ben and I
slept out in our backyard.
I said, "Let's count the stars tonight,
it shouldn't be too hard."

I started counting from the left;
Ben started on the right.
I knew we'd get them numbered
even if it took all night.

It wasn't long before I heard
my little brother snoring;
I guess he found that counting stars
could be a little boring.

I started over several times
because I'd lose my place.
It isn't easy keeping track
of all the stars in space.

I think I fin'lly fell asleep
a little after three.
How many stars are in the sky?
Don't ask me!

**God promised Abraham that he'd have
more descendants than there are stars
in the sky! See Genesis 15:5.**

No Kiddin'

It's just—Haw-Haw!—hysterical.
  It's so—Ho-Ho!—absurd.
    The most ridiculous—Tee-Hee!—thing
      I—Ha!—have ever heard.

        It's too—Hoo-Hoo!—hilarious
      and so—Ho-Ho!—outrageous.
    God said we're having a baby boy?
  Did he—Hee!—forget our ages?

    For I am nearly ninety
      and Abe, you're ninety-nine.
        Surely he can see that we
          are near the finish line.

          Maybe he was kiddin'
        when he said we'd have a son;
      it could be he was jokin'
    just to have a little fun.

No, you say, this is the truth—
    it's not a silly rumor.
        I guess I didn't think that God
          had such a sense of humor.

What will we call our little one?
Whom shall we name him after?
What's that you say?
You have a name?
You want to call him Laughter?!

**Abraham and Sarah named their son Isaac,
which is the Hebrew word for "laughter."
See Genesis 18:10-15; 21:1-7.**

Where Are We Goin'?

"Where are we goin'?"
little Isaac asked his pop.
"Are ya gonna take me fishin'
or to the candy shop?"

"Why are you so silent?
Have you planned a big surprise?
Are you keepin' it a secret?
Should I cover up my eyes?"

"When will we get there?
How much longer till we stop?
Are we gonna climb that mountain?
Are we hikin' to the top?"

"What will we do there
when we finally reach the peak?
Say, Pop,
is that a teardrop
that is rollin' down your cheek?"

Why was Isaac's dad so sad? Read Genesis 22.

Rebekah's Trek

I have bumped, I have bounced
back and forth, up and down
on the hump of this big ol' beast.
We have lumbered along for umpteen days
since leaving my home back east.

I am not complainin'—
    I am glad to go to Canaan,
        for I get to meet the man I'm gonna marry.
        But I'm so saddle-sore,
            and it truly is a bore
            caravannin' on a drooling dromedary.

But soon we'll have a wedding,
and I bet I'll be forgetting
all the miles that
I traveled on this brute.
And this trip will be worthwhile
when I see my Isaac smile
(especially if he's really, really cute).

Read about love and camels in Genesis 24.

Birthright Broth

Esau was a nitwit—
a silly nincompoop—
he sold his whole inheritance
for just a bowl of soup.

Now don't you act like Esau
and trade the whole caboodle
just because your brother says
he'll make some chicken noodle.

wanna
trade?

**Why did Esau do that?
Read about it in
Genesis 25:27-34.**

Jacob's Lament

Rachel is mad at Bilhah
'cause Bilhah never helps around the house.
Bilhah is upset with Leah,
since Leah spilled some grape juice on her blouse.
Leah's really irked with Zilpah
'cause Zilpah never cleans up when she cooks.
Zilpah cannot tolerate Rachel,
she's always giving Rachel dirty looks.
Rachel is disgusted with Leah,
she says she doesn't do her share of chores.
Leah is perturbed with Bilhah
'cause she really hates the way that Bilhah snores.

Bilhah's awfully miffed with Zilpah
'cause she leaves the bathroom in a mess.
Zilpah is outraged with Rachel
'cause Rachel didn't ask to wear her dress.

My tent is always filled with tons of tension—
so thick that you could cut it with a knife.
My problems are too plentiful to mention
since I went and wed more than one wife!

Wrestling Match

Jake was awakened
in the middle of the night
by a tall strappin' stranger
looking for a fight.
Now Jake wasn't one
to ever back down,
so soon those two
were agrapplin' on the ground.

Scramblin' and scrappin',
tusslin' and tumblin'—
musclin' with all their might.
Scufflin' and strugglin',
wrastlin' and rumblin'—
It was a knock-down, drag-out fight.

On and on, with all their brawn
they brawled all through the night—
carryin' on till the crack of dawn—
then stopped when they saw daylight.

But Jake held on to the stranger's foot
and said, "Whoa-ho-ho-ho!
Unless you bless my life right now
I will not let you go!"

The stranger was an angel,
and changed ol' Jacob's name;
and from that day this Israel
was never quite the same.

**Find this gripping tale
in Genesis 32:22-32.**

Joseph's Fashion Show

Brother Reuben, see my brand-new robe?
Brother Judah, look how I am dressed.
Brother Levi, dig my cool clothes.
Simeon, I see you are impressed.

Issachar and Zebulun, I know you will agree,
your little brother never looked so good.
And Gad and Naphtali, you know you'll never see
a finer jacket in this neighborhood.

Oh, aren't I dashing, Asher?
And aren't I dapper, Dan?
I guess that's why they always say
that clothes make the man!

Find out his brothers' reaction to Joseph's cool clothes in Genesis 37:4.

Brother 4 Sale

Confession

Joe's big brothers did a terrible thing,
a dirty deed that I would NEVER do.
OK, I will be honest,
all right, I will admit,
I'd like to sell my little brother too!

Did Joseph's older
brothers really sell him?
See Genesis 37:28.

Dreamer

I've always been a dreamer,
I dream my life away—
at least that's what my parents
and my teachers always say.

'Cause when I do my schoolwork,
my mind will often stray
and dream of all the cool things
I know I'll do someday.

Young Joseph was a dreamer;
his folks got flustered too.
But in the end they sure were glad
that all his dreams came true.

We need more kids like Joseph,
with spiritual eyes to see
all the wonderfully awesome things
that still are yet to be!

What did Joseph dream about? Find out in Genesis 37:6-9.

Family Reunion

Remember me?
It's little Joe—
your pesky, bratty, little bro,
the kid you sold for twenty bucks
so many, many years ago.

Don't feel bad for sellin' me—
I'm fine with it because I know
that all of this was meant to be
so God could save our family.

No, I surely didn't have
an easy childhood,
but what you meant for evil
God has turned around for good!

**Did Joseph really forgive his brothers?
Find out in Genesis 45:1-15.**

Baby Moses

Itty-bitty baby,
bundled in a blanket,
bobbing in a basket
on the river Nile.

Itty-bitty baby,
don't ya make a racket
or you could be a snack
for a crocodile.

What happened?
Find out in Exodus 2:1-10.

Speechless

O Lord, you m-must be jokin',
you know I'm t-too soft-spoken,
I'm not the type to t-talk before a crowd.
You'd b-better find another—
how ab-bout my big ol' brother?
For his booming voice is b-big and b-bold and loud.

Lord, I'd do it if I c-could,
you know I surely w-would,
but my voice is kinda wh-whiny and w-weak.
I'd be m-misunderstood
'cause my grammar ain't so good,
and I always st-st-stammer when I speak.

With my t-tummy all aflutter,
I would only sp-spit and sp-sputter,
and the sentences I utter
would be n-nothin' but a m-mutter,
like my m-mouth was all aclutter
with a p-pound of p-peanut butter.
Oh, I wish I didn't st-stutter,
but I . . .
W-what's that you say?
You're g-gonna use me anyway?

See what God told Moses in Exodus 4:10-17.

Countdown

Moses spoke with the ol' Pharaoh
and told him, "Let my people go!"
But Pharaoh shook his head and said,
"No!"

So God turned the water into icky red blood—
every river and lake was thicker than mud.
The fish bellied up and rotted on the shore,
and no one ever smelled such a stench before.

Chorus

Moses went back to the ol' Pharaoh
and told him, "Let my people go!"
But Pharaoh shook his head and said,
"No!"

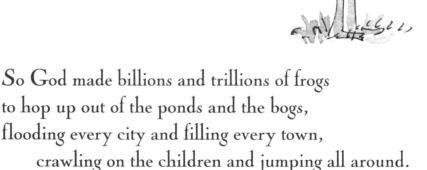

So God made billions and trillions of frogs
to hop up out of the ponds and the bogs,
flooding every city and filling every town,
crawling on the children and jumping all around.

Repeat Chorus

So God turned the dust into little black gnats—
the kind that get under your shirts and your hats
to nibble on your arms and whine in your ears—
enough to bring anyone to tears.

Repeat Chorus

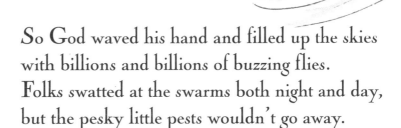

So God waved his hand and filled up the skies
with billions and billions of buzzing flies.
Folks swatted at the swarms both night and day,
but the pesky little pests wouldn't go away.

Repeat Chorus

So God caused a terrible disease to spread,
and all the livestock just dropped dead:
mounds of cows and heaps of sheep,
piles of camels 20 feet deep!

Repeat Chorus

So God touched the people with miserable sores,
and no one could do their daily chores,
for dads and moms and teens and tots
just sat and scratched their itchy spots.

Repeat Chorus

So God sent hailstones and big raindrops
that flattened the fields and ruined the crops.
It crumpled the corn and wrecked the wheat,
so there was nothing left to eat.

Repeat Chorus

So God stirred a wind to blow from the east
that blew in locusts to make a feast
of every last leaf on every last tree;
great grasshoppers gobbled the greenery.

Repeat Chorus

So God ordered darkness to cover the land,
and a man couldn't see his very own hand.
The desert sun refused to blaze,
and there was no light for three long days.

Repeat Chorus

So God brought one last tragedy
that jolted every family.
Egyptian parents screamed and cried
as they found their oldest sons had died.

Pharaoh said to Moses now,
"This time I won't say no.
Take every last person, sheep, and cow,
and go! Go! Go! Go! Go!"

Read about the ten plagues in Exodus 7–12.

Invasion of the Swamp Creatures

Can you imagine what life would be like
if frogs took over your town?
If billions of bouncing amphibians
turned everything upside down?
It'd be a froggy free-for-all,
a frenzied, frantic sight
fraught with much frustration,
much friction, and much fright.
Frogs would storm the schools,
and frogs would flood the mall;
they'd swarm in all the swimming pools
and overrun city hall.

The pests would infest the houses,
the pests would congest the streets;
they'd rest upon your pillow
and nest between your sheets.
Frogs would clog the freeways,
and frogs would block the bridges;
they'd overflow the ovens
and fill up all the fridges.

MOVE IT!!!

They'd backstroke in your bathtub
and paddle in your sink;
   they'd dive into your water glass
      while you try to take a drink.
         They'd never cease to stare at you
            with great big bulging eyes
               while sitting on your burger
                  and nibbling on your fries.
                     But if you're gonna have a plague
                        I guess that frogs are fine—
                           it'd be a whole lot worse to have
                              a plague of porcupines.

Supersize, everyone!

This toad-ally happened!
Read about it in Exodus 8.

Small Problem

These teeny-tiny gnats
are drivin' me nuts!
These teeny-tiny gnats are naughty.
These teeny-tiny gnats
get through my nets
and nibble all over my body.
These teeny-tiny gnats
are causing knots
to gnarl up in my tummy.
Oh, how many days
and how many nights
will gnats think I am yummy?!

Just a Few Things

It's just a few things for the journey—
they say this trek may take a week or two.
We're leaving Egypt first thing in the morning—
I've got a lot of packing left to do!

I'm gonna need to get some extra boxes
for all the stuff I'll have to have on hand.
There won't be time to stop and do some shopping
until we settle in the promised land.

My hubby won't be happy when he sees this—
my luggage piled higher than his ears.
He's gonna flip, and then I know he'll ask me,
"You think this trip'll take us forty years?"

**Read Exodus 12:31-38 and find out what the Israelites
took when they left Egypt.**

95

Old Man and the Sea

Since the beginning of history,
man has sought to cross the sea,
longing to reach the other shore—
to go where none has gone before.

Vikings, Pilgrims, and Eskimos,
Columbus, Magellan, and Cook
all boarded a boat so they could go
and have a closer look.

By catamaran or bamboo raft,
by schooner, skiff, or canoe—
sailors have sailed all kinds of craft
across the ocean blue.

Now Moses was no sailor—
he didn't own an oar—
but he performed a nautical feat
that none had done before.

For Moses crossed the big Red Sea
and reached the opposite shore
by walking on his own two feet
across the ocean floor.

**How'd he do that?
Look in Exodus 14:15-22.**

Don't Mess with Moses!

Don't mess with Moses
no matter what you do;
don't make the same mistake that Pharaoh made.
Don't mess with Moses
if you know what's good for you;
don't forget the price that Pharaoh paid.

His horses and his chariots,
his mighty men of war
were chasing all the Israelites
across the ocean floor
when all at once the army heard
a loud and fright'ning roar,
and Pharaoh's finest fighting force
was suddenly no more!

So don't mess with Moses
like those Egyptian guys—
what fools they were in all their fuss and fervor!
No, don't mess with Moses
(but if you feel you must,
I would suggest you wear a life preserver).

Check this story out in Exodus 14:23-31.

A New Song
and Dance

I'm Moses' sister Miriam.
I love to sing and dance,
to belt out a tune
at the top of my lungs,
to leap to my feet and prance.
I'm never one to hesitate
when it is time to celebrate,
and now it seems
I have the perfect chance.

For God used brother Moses
    to set his people free
        from years and years
            of bitter tears and cruel slavery.
    So now it's time to party
    and to shout the victory,
for there lies Pharaoh's army
at the bottom of the sea.

    I'm gonna shake my tambourine
        and sing a brand-new song
            (the words are in Exodus 15
                if you'd like to sing along).

Find the song in Exodus 15:20, 21.

Manna

Manna for breakfast,
manna for brunch,
and yes, you guessed it,
manna for lunch.

But Mama promised
(if we aren't naughty)
tonight she'll make us
some manna-cotti.

**Read about this heavenly
food in Exodus 16.**

Rock Springs

Whack, whack, whack!
With his walking stick
Moses smacked the side of the mountain.

Whoosh, whoosh, whoosh!
Through a crack in the rock
came the world's first drinking fountain!

What was that place called? Find out in Exodus 17:7.

God Rules

Only fools
ignore the rules—
I'm sure you never would.
You understand
that God's commands
are always for your good!

What ten rules did God give Moses?
Look them up in Exodus 20:1-17.

Golden Calves

I find it kinda funny,
it sorta makes me laugh—
that tale about the crowd that bowed
before a golden calf.

I really think it's humorous
the things that people do—
how folks will bow before a cow
that cannot even moo.

For who would want to worship
an object made of gold—
a god that cannot walk or talk
or heal a common cold?

Still folks today are just the same
as those that lived before.
We seem to choose some silly stuff
to worship and adore,

like fancy cars and movie stars,
like money, gold, or fame—
some worship sports of every sort
or a favorite video game.

But there is only one true God
worthy to be adored.
Let's be faithful to worship him—
our maker and our Lord.

What were those Israelites thinking?
Read about it in Exodus 32.

Laying Down the Law

We learned today in Sunday school
how Moses goes and blows his cool.
He throws the Ten Commandments down—
a grandiose explosion on the ground!

My teacher only glared at me
as if I were a dunce
when I asked if this meant Moses
broke all ten commands at once!

What did Moses do next? See Exodus 32:19, 20.

Fault Line

Korah and his cohorts were not humble—
to Moses they were nothing but a pain.
All they did was murmur, moan, and mumble—
they'd criticize and constantly complain.

Now Korah and his cohorts never grumble—
ever since that earthquake took its toll.
For on that day the ground began to rumble,
then opened up and swallowed them whole!

This really happened! Read about it in Numbers 16.

Why?–ners

Those folks that fled from Pharaoh
gave Moses a lot o' flak.
These are the things those whiners spoke
to his face and behind his back:

"Why can't we just go back home to Egypt?"
"Why did we ever have to leave?"
"Why must we obey every little word you say?"
"Oh, what will all this craziness achieve?"

"Why must we only munch on manna?"
"Why can't we ever lunch on leeks?"
"And why have we wandered in this wilderness
for weeks and weeks and weeks and weeks?"

c'mon... why?

Moses grew so weary of their whining;
he'd had enough of hearing them bemoan.
Moses said, "Now listen to me, people,
for I have got some whys of my own."

"Why would you want to live in Egypt?
Why would you want to be a slave?
Why would you want to work your fingers to the bone
every day until you're lyin' in your grave?"

"Why would you like to be in bondage?
Why would you choose to live in chains?
Can't you understand
we can have the promised land?
Oh, when will all you whiners use your brains?!"

(I hope that I grow up to be like Moses—
I don't wanna be a whiner like the rest.
For I am sure the Bible says God chose us
to know him and believe him for the best.)

Donkey Talk

Next time you hear a donkey talk,
much to your dismay,
it's probably best you heed the beast
and let him have his way.
A donkey rarely ever speaks—
he'd really rather bray—
unless there's something significant
that "hee haws" to say!

**Read about the talking donkey
in Numbers 22.**

Fightin' Chants

Everyone knows
(as the saying goes)
you can't fight city hall.
And so instead
ol' Joshua said,
"Let's try the city wall!"

Wall of Sound

The Hebrew children were seen, not heard,
outside the walls of Jericho.
They did not speak a single word
for six days in a row.

But finally, on the seventh day,
they couldn't hold their tongues;
as trumpets blasted they began
to shout at the top of their lungs.

The walls began to rumble—
they rattled, rocked, and rolled.
Their stones began to crumble—
the fortress was about to fold.

The folks inside the city walls trembled
as God's people made a deafening sound.
Jericho was quickly disassembled
as the walls came acrashin' to the ground.

So, children, we can learn a lasting lesson
from that earsplitting Hebrew crowd:
though you're told it is good to be quiet,
sometimes it is better to be LOUD!

This exciting story is told in Joshua 6.

Time Warp

God made the sun stand perfectly still
by stopping Earth's rotation.
I wish he'd try that next July
and stretch my summer vacation.

Look in Joshua 10 and
find out why Joshua prayed
for the sun to stop.

A Woman's Place

Some say a woman's place is in the kitchen—
apparently the Lord does not agree.
If Deb'rah had stayed home to do the dishes,
her army would've lost the victory!

Read about this judge of Israel in Judges 4.

Jael

Jael was a gutsy gal—
a hero some have said.
Her scheme to save God's people
hit the nail right on the head!

What did she do? Find out in Judges 4:15-24.

120

Boondoggled

You can't win a battle
by bustin' big ol' bottles—
so Gideon, you better guess again.
No, you can't win a battle
by blastin' on those bugles—
besides you only have 300 men!
You can't win a battle
by blabbering some babble
and bellowing as boldly as you can.
Your battle will be boggled—
it's bound to be boondoggled—
unless you have a better battle plan!

Did this plan work for Gideon?
Read about it in Judges 7.

no sword?

Tough Love

I have a real good buddy—
he's very strong and tough.
But often he forgets his strength
and plays a little rough.

Every time he shakes my hand
he makes my knuckles crack.
He always knocks me over
when he slaps me on the back.

He's only being friendly
when he hugs me like a bear,
but squeezes tight with all his might
until I have no air!

I really love my buddy—
I'll be faithful to the end.
But man, it can be painful
having Samson for a friend.

Samson's story is told in Judges 13-16.

Pumping Iron

Samson found no challenge
in merely lifting weights—
I'm sure you've heard
he much preferred
lifting city gates.

See Judges 16:3.

Hair–Razing Tale

Samson was so stout and strong
while his locks were thick and long,

but all his strength came to a stop
when Miss Delilah trimmed his mop.

(So here's the perfect tale to share
when your dad says "CUT YOUR HAIR!")

Find out what Delilah did in Judges 16:17-21.

I'm just trying to be like Samson...

125

In-Law Lessons

Ruth was never rude to her mother-in-law.
Ruth was always kind and good.
She wasn't on the lookout for every little flaw
but loved her like her own daughter would.

Why can't you be more like Ruth?

I'm sure she wasn't absolutely perfect,
but if you really want to know the truth,
I think there is a whole gob of grown-ups
that could learn a little thing or two from Ruth.

Read about Ruth and her in-laws in Ruth 1 and 2.

Sleepyhead

Little Sammy Sleepyhead—
dozin' in his cozy bed.
Someone spoke, so Sammy woke,
for this is what that someone said: "Samuel."

Sammy jumped up on his feet
and started down the hall,
saying, "Eli, here I am.
I think I heard you call."

"Silly Sammy," Eli said,
"turn around, go back to bed.
Any word you may have heard
was only in your head."

So down the hall young Sammy sped—
he soon was snoozing in his bed.
Someone spoke, again he woke,
for this is what that someone said: "Samuel."

So Sammy jumped up on his feet
and started down the hall,
saying, "Eli, here I am.
I'm *sure* I heard you call?"

"Sammy, Sammy," Eli said,
"I thought I told you—back to bed!
Don't you see some silly dream
is floating in your head?"

So down the hall young Sammy sped—
he soon was snoozing in his bed.
Someone spoke, again he woke,
for this is what that someone said: "Samuel."

So Sammy jumped up on his feet
and started down the hall,
shouting, "Eli, here I am!
I KNOW I heard you call!"

**What did the Lord say
to Samuel?
Read 1 Samuel 3:11-14.**

By now ol' Eli figured out
that this was not a game.
He said to Sam, "I think I know
who's calling out your name."

"Go back to bed, but now instead
of closing your eyelids,
open your ears so you may hear—
God often talks to kids."

Old King Saul

Old King Saul
was a sorry old soul
with a heart so cold and jealous.
Saul's sad life doesn't end so well—
so what's his story tell us?

**Read about the start of Saul's troubles
in 1 Samuel 15:24-29.**

Hotshot

David is a sharpshootin' shepherd—
he is mighty handy with a sling.
He can hit a lion or a leopard—
fact is, he can hit most anything.

David is a sharpshootin' shepherd—
he is mighty handy with a sling.
But if you think he's skillful with a weapon,
you should hear that hotshot sing!

David was a good athlete and an excellent musician. See 1 Samuel 16:18.

Fit for a King

Today the prophet Samuel turned up in our hometown
to say that one of my own sons would one day wear a crown.
He said, "Hey, Jesse, call your boys—God'll make it known
which child of yours is truly fit to reign upon the throne."
So naturally, I thought the Lord would choose my oldest son.
Eliab is my brightest boy—by far the boldest one.
But as my firstborn strutted by with such a regal sway,
the prophet only shook his head and said to me, "No way!"

I thought, *Maybe Abinadab, the second son in line,*
will make a grand impression 'cause that boy is dressed so fine.
But Samuel took one look at him and gave him two thumbs-down.
The old man said, "Too bad his head's too big to wear the crown."
I knew it must be Shammah then, my offspring number three,
for he is such a handsome man and looks like royalty.
But Samuel only rolled his eyes and looked down at the floor.
He said, "I'm sorry, but he's not the guy God's looking for."

My fourth son is so studly that I truly was perplexed—
Samuel hardly glanced at him and simply shouted, "Next!"
Son number five did not survive the man of God's inspection.
Son number six was quickly nixed and slunk off in rejection.
My seventh son had barely stood, when we all heard, "Not!"
Then Samuel turned to me and said, "So who else ya got?"

"Just my youngest, David," I responded with a grunt,
"but he is not the kingly kind—he's nothin' but a runt.
He plays the harp, he loves to sing,
and he can swing the meanest sling.
But I don't know a single thing
that makes me think he could be king."

The old man said, "Go fetch the kid."
So that's exactly what we did.
When Samuel saw my last-born son,
God whispered to him, "He's the one."
The prophet poured anointing oil all over David's head.
Then pointing to our future king, he told us what God said,
"Human sight is not enough—our eyes see just a part.
We only view the outside—God can look *inside* the heart."

Read this story in 1 Samuel 16.

Giant Size

If Goliath were alive today
he could be a center for the **NBA**—
the guy was over 9 feet tall!
He'd be a natural at basketball.

With height like his,
he would be hot—
I bet he'd never miss a shot.
The man would dominate the sport—
a superstar out on the court.

He'd be elected
to the **Hall of Fame**—
the **MVP** of every game.
He'd be the envy of all the teams—
the answer to his coach's dreams.

I think it's such a tragedy
there was no b-ball in 1000 BC,
'cause giants would've had
something better to do
than pickin' on kids
like me and you.

Who did Goliath pick on?
Find out in 1 Samuel 17.

Saul's Armor

"Here, young man, put this on,"
commanded big King Saul.
"Surely, son, you realize
wearing my armor would be wise.
Goliath's more than twice your size—
I hear he's 10 feet tall."

David tried the armor on,
it didn't fit at all,
for king-size Saul wore extra large
while David took a small.

With a heavy-metal jacket
and a helmet on his head,
David knew he couldn't move
and he'd be as good as dead.

So, taking off the hand-me-downs,
he turned to Saul and said,
"No thanks, my king,
I'll bring my sling
and trust the Lord instead."

Read about this in 1 Samuel 17:38, 39.

Dog Fight

David gathered five smooth stones
down at the babblin' brook,
then headed toward Goliath
with his sling and shepherd's crook.

He stood before the giant
with the slingshot and the staff
as Goliath started houndin' him
with a great big husky laugh.

"What is this? Some skinny kid
with nuttin' but a stick?
And I must be some mangy mutt
he thinks that he can lick."

(I guess that's just exactly what
the little shepherd thought,
judgin' from the beatin'
that the big ol' giant got.)

That puppy got a big surprise
when he was struck between the eyes—
the poor ol' pooch, once so robust,
just hit the dirt and bit the dust.

I guess Goliath spoke the truth,
he'd figured it out, all right.
Indeed he was a dirty dog—
with a bark worse than his bite!

Read this true story in 1 Samuel 17:40-51.

Last Words

"I'm gonna feed your flesh to the birds."
(These are Goliath's famous last words.)

See 1 Samuel 17:44.

Friends

David and Jonathan
were often found
just hangin' together
and messin' around,
actin' kind o' crazy,
like a couple o' clowns,
by teasing each other
or tusslin' on the ground.

While shootin' arrows
or skipping rocks,
these two had their share
of heart-to-heart talks;
like brother to brother
they both would confide
by tellin' each other
what was happ'nin' inside.

Jon was not
just a fair-weather friend—
he was true to David
down to the end.
He showed his love with loyalty—
now that's the kind of buddy
that I want to be.

Read about these pals in 1 Samuel 18:1-4; 20.

Dancin' Dave

Dancin' Dave, Dancin' Dave,
is that any way for a king to behave?
Twistin' and twirlin' in the public square,
swayin' and swirlin' in the open air,
wheelin' and whirlin' like you don't even care
that you're dressed in nothin'
but your underwear.

Dancin' Dave, Dancin' Dave,
really! Must you rant and rave?
Singin' and shoutin' out in plain sight,
bobbin' and bouncin' in broad daylight
as if you're announcin' that it's really all right
to worship the Lord with all your might.

Dancin' Dave, Dancin' Dave,
I have to admit you truly are brave.
You don't hold back
when you praise your maker—
no wonder they say
you're a mover and shaker!

Why did David dance?
Read 2 Samuel 6:12-23.

Absalom

Absalom was a handsome prince
  with a head full of beautiful curls.
    Perfectly styled, his hair was piled
    much higher than any girl's.

Not only was his hair poofed up,
  his pride was puffed up too;
    the pompous prince, so self-impressed,
    was proud of his poodle-do.

While galloping through the woods one day,
  as he was waging war,
    a leafy limb reached out to him
      and grabbed his pompadour.

Of course his horse was startled
and left him dangling there.
The proud young man then met his end,
hanging by his hair.

If Absalom were here right now,
I'm sure that he would say
that his was the first
(and the world's very worst)
BAD HAIR DAY!

**You can read about this
character in 2 Samuel 18.**

David's Diary

King David kept a diary—
it did his spirit good
to jot his thoughts and feelings down
every chance he could.

At times he wrote down praises,
sometimes composed a prayer;
he scribbled his frustrations
when life seemed so unfair.

He wrote when he was happy,
he wrote when he was sad;
he wrote down the impressions
and the questions that he had.

You can read his journal—
it's **OK** to take a look—
just turn in your Bible
to the middle of the book.

**David and others wrote down
their feelings in the Psalms.**

The Lord Is My Shepherd

The Lord is my shepherd,
and I am his sheep
(though I never bleat
or grow wool).
This is one way to say
my God always keeps
me warm and safe and full.

Read more in Psalm 23.

Thirsty Deer

Last night I watched a nature show
on channel 55.
It told about a thirsty doe
that struggled to survive.

She wandered in a barren land
that saw no rain for weeks,
and where the cruel blazing sun
dried up the pools and creeks.

...Ahhhhhh!

Her body was weak, her throat was parched,
her lips were cracked and dry.
She knew she must find water soon
or she would surely die.

At last she reached a quiet stream
and plunged into a pool;
the water tasted wonderful,
the water felt so cool.

O God, my soul is like that doe,
for it is thirsty too.
It doesn't pant for water though—
it longs for more of you.

Read about being thirsty in Psalm 42.

Heart Praise

You can teach a parrot
to repeat "Praise the Lord!"
You can train an ape
to put his arms up in the air.
You can get a poodle to
roll over on the floor,
and ev'ry travelin' circus
has a big ol' dancing bear.

It's wonderful to sing and dance
or clap your hands and shout,
but what is happenin' in the heart
is what it's all about.

"With all my heart I will praise you, O Lord my God. I will give glory to your name forever." Psalm 86:12

Wonderfully Made

When I look at my reflection in the mirror,
   I'd have to say I'm really not impressed.
     I wish that my complexion was much clearer;
      I'd love to be a whole lot better dressed.

       I wish that I was thinner in the middle
        so I could fit into the coolest clothes.
        I wish my hair was long,
          I wish my arms were strong,
        I wish there were no freckles on my nose.

       I wish I had no pimples on my forehead
     and didn't have these dimples on my chin.
    I wish my teeth were straight,
   I wish I'd lose some weight,
I wish I had no scratches on my skin.

   I wish my knees were not so big and knobby
    and that my feet were not so pigeon-toed.
      I wish my ears were small,
       I wish that I was tall,
        I wish my bony legs were not so bowed.

And when I'm finally finished feeling sorry for myself,
  at the end of my very long tirade,
    God gently whispers to my heart once again,
      "You are fearfully and wonderfully made."

Read Psalm 139 to find out what God thinks about you.

Whiz Kid

People call King Solomon "The World's Wisest Man."
The Bible boasts of brilliant things he did.
It makes me kinda curious—I wanna understand
what Sol was like when he was just a kid.

I bet he was a genius from the moment of his birth—
the greatest child prodigy that ever lived on earth.
He learned the Hebrew alphabet while he was in his bassinette,
and at the tender age of three he prob'ly had a PhD.

He studied physics in first grade, and calculus in third,
and won the national spelling bee with a fifty-letter word.
He always paid attention, and he never broke a rule;
he never got detention or had to stay after school.

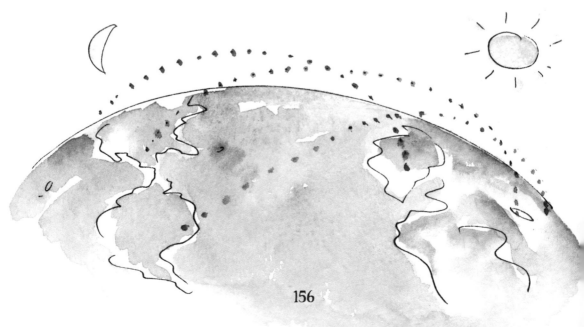

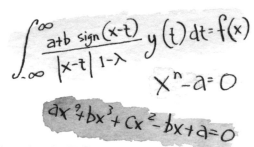

$$\int_{-\infty}^{\infty} \frac{a+b\;\text{sign}(x-t)}{|x-t|\;1-\lambda}\;y(t)\,dt = f(x)$$

$$x^n - a = 0$$

$$ax^9 + bx^3 + cx^2 - bx + a = 0$$

Young Sol was blessed with a high **IQ**;
we would've been wowed with the facts he knew,
like the square root of sixty-nine trillion and two
or how many people play pool in **Peru**.

Although I could never compete with this kid,
I know I can do what King Solomon did—
he prayed for the wisdom to know what to do,
and I can pray that same way too.

**Wise up about this wise king
in 1 Kings 3 and 4.**

Split Decision

"This child is mine!"
a woman whined,
"I'm sure as sure can be."
"You're out of your mind!"
another cried,
"This baby belongs to me."
"He's mine!"
"Is not!"
"Is too!"
"Is not!"
And back and forth
the women fought
until King Solomon took the tot
and said, "Here's what we'll do . . ."

The wise king knew how he could see
just whose that baby was.
Tune in to 1 Kings, chapter 3
to find out what he does.

Writer's Cramp

Not only did King Solomon
have seven hundred wives,
he also had three hundred concubines.
So was it customary,
in the month of February,
for the king to send
a thousand valentines?

Was God happy about Solomon's women?
Look in 1 Kings 11:2, 3 and find out!

Rain Man

The Lord gave Elijah special power
to make every rain cloud go away.
Boy, I bet the folks up in Seattle
wish Elijah was alive today!

**Why did God take the rain away from
King Ahab's land? Read 1 Kings 16:30-33
and you'll see.**

Raven~ous

Elijah had to hide out in the desert;
he waited there for weeks and weeks and weeks.
He was fed by a flock of friendly ravens,
flying by with bits of bread in their beaks.

This story of Elijah really happened,
though I know it sounds completely absurd
that a man could survive, and somehow even thrive,
when for months he only ate like a bird.

Did Elijah really go to the birds? Read about it in 1 Kings 17:2-7.

Showdown

Hello, fans! We're here today
at the Carmel Sports Arena
to witness the showdown of the century.
Stay tuned right here—
don't touch that dial—
for this is a game
we know you'll want to see.

On one side stands Elijah—
the mighty man of God.
He's up against the prophets of Baal—
a four-hundred-and-fifty-man squad.

Each side will offer a sacrifice,
invoking their "higher power."
The winner will be the side whose god
responds with firepower!

This contest is quite important;
the outcome will surely reveal
once and for all—Jehovah or Baal—
which god is really real?

Team Baal has won the coin toss;
it looks like they'll lead out.
Their team is looking confident;
they seem to have no doubt.

Their offering's on the altar;
they're acting so devout.
Look at 'em pray—*zzzzzzzzt!*
Hear 'em—*zzzzzzzt*—and shout!

Uh-oh, folks, it looks like we
are having some techni—*zzzzt*—difficulty.
Don't try to adjust—*zzzzt*—
it's not—*zzzzzzzt*—your TV.

I guess you'll need—*zzzzzt*—
to tune in to 1 Kings 18
　　　to find out—*zzzzt*—
　　　　　which side—*zzzt*—
　　　　　　　will win this—*zzt*—
　　　　　　　　　famous bout.

Don't You Be Like Jezebel

Don't you be like Jezebel,
that queen was mean and rude.
Don't you be like Jezebel,
forever in a mood.
Don't you be like Jezebel,
or have her attitude.
(Unless you wish to wind up as
a dish of doggie food!)

What happened to this wicked queen?
Read about her end in 2 Kings 9.

Speedy King Jehu

Speedy King Jehu
drove like mad—
just a little slower
than my own granddad!

How is Jehu's driving described in 2 Kings 9:20?

King Rehoboam

If King Rehoboam had eighty-eight kids,
how could he remember all their names?
And how did Rehoboam
find the time to get to know 'em,
and go to all of their baseball games?

Find out a few of their names in 2 Chronicles 11:18-22.

Battle Hymn

Mighty King Jehoshaphat
sent us into war,
armed with a secret weapon
that we'd never used before.

No bow and arrow,
no sword or shield
was even brought along.
Instead we marched
on the battlefield
with nothing but a song.

Singing is for sissies, I thought,
this battle plan's all wrong.
But I joined in with the rest of them
and sang out loud and strong.

they don't look so tough now, do they?

As we began the chorus
"Give thanks for God is good,"
our enemies fled before us,
making tracks as fast as they could.

The bad guys simply scattered,
and we hadn't rattled a sword;
instead we had lifted our voices
and left the battle to the Lord.

I learned a powerful lesson
on the battlefield that day:
singin' ain't for sissies,
no matter what they say!

**Check this out in
2 Chronicles 20:20-30.**

Boil in oil,
then off with her head!

A Royal Pain

We Israelites
weren't thinkin' right
the day we demanded a king.
We didn't consider
how life would be bitter
from troubles
a tyrant would bring.

Did we forget
when kings are upset
they yell at the drop of a hat,
"Off with his head!"
and "Boil her in oil!"
and gruesome things like that!

Queen Esther's Quest

The Jews were in a dreadful mess;
they'd soon be dead, that is unless
Queen Esther met with good success and set her people free.
So Esther dressed in her Sunday best
and prayed the king would be impressed
as she delivered her request before His Majesty.

"I must confess," the queen expressed,
"I'm just a little bit distressed;
the king detests unscheduled guests,
and that includes his wife.
But still I will not ever rest
until this thing is off my chest—
my fellow Jews I choose to bless, though I may lose my life."

Will Esther pass this stressful test?
And will the king grant her request?
Or will he think she's just a pest
and have his guards arrest her?
Will the king say no or yes?
I think it's anybody's guess.
So if you've got to know the rest,
go read the book of Esther!

**For the short story,
read Esther 5:1-4; 7.**

Lean Green Cuisine

Daniel loves his vegetables,
that's all he ever eats.
He never gobbles goodies;
he never swallows sweets.

He likes to crunch on carrots
and munch on mustard greens.
For breakfast he has brussels sprouts;
his lunch is lima beans.

At suppertime it's spinach;
dessert is broccoli;
and for a healthy bedtime snack,
a stalk of celery.

He never chooses chocolate cake
like all the other guys.
He seems to think his veggies make
him much more strong and wise!

**Believe it or not, this is true!
Check it out in Daniel 1:8-17.**

Shadrach, Meshach, and Abednego

Shadrach, Meshach, and Abednego
were told to bow
when the horns would blow.
But those boys
ignored the noise.
"We only kneel to the God we know,"
said Shadrach, Meshach, and Abednego.

Shadrach, Meshach, and Abednego
would not give in
to the status quo.
"We will not fold
to a god of gold
just because the king says so,"
said Shadrach, Meshach, and Abednego.

Shadrach, Meshach, and Abednego
enraged the king
when they told him, "No."
They declined
to change their minds,
so into the blazing inferno
went Shadrach, Meshach, and Abednego.

Shadrach, Meshach, and Abednego—
engulfed in flames
from head to toe.
Those Israelites
would not ignite,
so there in the fire, to and fro,
went Shadrach, Meshach, and Abednego.

Shadrach, Meshach, and Abednego
kept cooler than
an Eskimo.
They didn't choke
or smell of smoke
but came out basking in the afterglow—
that Shadrach, Meshach, and Abednego.

How did they escape the fire? This cool story is in Daniel 3.

Fourth Man

We counted four fellows in the furnace—
footloose and fancy-free.
There's one little thing
that does concern us—
we only threw in three!

This is all so puzzling and perplexing.
Please help us solve the mystery.
How about you?
Do you have a clue
just who that extra man could be?

**Hmmm, who do you think
that fourth man is?
See Daniel 3:25, 28.**

Miracles

Old Moses saw a miracle
the day the ocean split;
young David saw a miracle
the day he made a "hit."

Balaam saw a miracle
the day his donkey spoke,
and a miracle kept Shadrach's life
from going up in smoke.

These men saw mighty miracles,
but Mom can toot her horn—
she says she saw a miracle
the day that I was born!

Finicky Felines

"How long till lunch?" roared Leon.
"A lion's gotta eat!
I need some crunchy bones to munch
and chunks of raw red meat!"

"I'm hungry too!" lamented Lou.
"I need some chow to chomp and chew—
something delicious, something nutritious,
something to sink my teeth into."

Then Loretta let out a roar,
"I cannot take it anymore!
My stomach's growling, my sides are sore—
meat is a must for a carnivore!"

The cats continued to carp and complain;
they snarled and gnarled and bared their fangs,
until at last a meal was brought
to ease their biting hunger pangs.

Down into the dingy den,
Daniel, their dinner, was dropped.
The lions lurched, the lions lunged,
but then . . . they suddenly stopped.

They whiffed and they sniffed their frightened food
from his head down to his toes.
Then each of the cats just walked away,
turning up its nose.

Apparently their roaring
was much worse than their bite,
for they found the menu boring
and they lost their appetite.

**Why did these cats refuse
their dinner? Find out
in Daniel 6:19-22.**

Purrfect Pillow

These poor accommodations
leave a lot to be desired;
they don't provide a blanket or a bed.
But though I'm pretty tired,
a bunk is not required,
for I've found the perfect place to rest my head.

The pillows here are fluffy—
quite cozy and quite comfy;
they're fashioned from the finest feline fur.
So as I lay me down to sleep,
I know the Lord my soul will keep,
as I listen to my pillow softly purr.

Read more about this guy in Daniel 6.

Bones

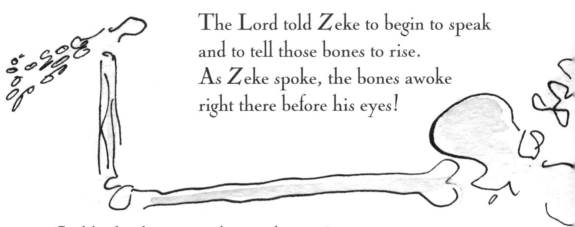

Zeke was standin' in the middle of a valley
that was littered with a billion ol' bones.
There were femurs and fibulas scattered with scapulas,
and skulls lined up like little tombstones.

The Lord told Zeke to begin to speak
and to tell those bones to rise.
As Zeke spoke, the bones awoke
right there before his eyes!

Suddenly they started to rattle,
they clanked and clattered and creaked.
Ezekiel was wantin' to skedaddle—
just imagine how he must have freaked!
For the sound from the shakin' of those brittle ol' bones
was like millions of marimbas and a zillion xylophones
makin' nightmarish music with their haunting hollow tones.

What happened next Zeke didn't expect,
for there in the middle of the noise,
all those lively ol' limbs then began to append,
end to end, just like Tinkertoys.

Toe bones connected to foot bones,
ankles were anchored to shins,
kneecaps attached to the thighbones
that hooked themselves up to the hips;
rib cages clamped onto spine bones,
jawbones were joined up to skulls,
arm bones were linked up to hand bones,
that fastened to five fingertips.

Right there and right then, every skeleton
was covered with muscle and skin,
till they looked once again like who they had been
a way, way, way back when.

The Lord then poured his Spirit out
and filled those bodies with breath;
they stood to their feet, now fully alive,
free from the power of death.
Just think, if God can give new life
to ribs and vertebrae,
you know he'll pour his Spirit out
on you and me today!

This spine-tingling tale is told in Ezekiel 37:1-14.

183

Bellyache

Oh, I got me a whale of a bellyache,
a pain in the pit of my tummy.
Something I ate was a big mistake
'cause boy, do I feel crummy!
There isn't any question—my problem's indigestion
from something that I swallowed, I presume.
I guess it's always best to watch what I ingest
and be careful of the creatures I consume.
I tasted a whole ton of tuna
and then, like a ravenous fool,
porked out on a big pod of porpoise
and scarfed squirmy squid by the school.
I ate a great deal of electric eel—
is that why I feel so queasy?
That mammoth meal of elephant seal
didn't go down so easy.
Was it the grunion with garlic and onion,
or was it the curried cod?
Perhaps the snapper with hot chili peppers
is making me feel so odd.
Was it the bowl of crab casserole,
or the big jug of jellyfish juice?

Was it the plate of skate that I ate,
or the big dish of mackerel mousse?
I'm sure it's dessert that is making me hurt,
for I feel like I'm gonna explode!
The angelfish cake must be making me ache,
or that fresh octo-pie à la mode.
I suppose that the swordfish, the sawfish, or spearfish
somehow got stuck in my throat.
I bet the great white was too big for one bite,
or how 'bout that 40-foot boat?
That clam chowder was delicious—I guess I got ambitious,
eating cup after cup after cup.
I should've been more cautious 'cause now I feel nauseous,
and I think that I'm gonna throw u—!

What did this poor fish eat?
Find out by reading Jonah 1 and 2.

Bible Names

Methuselah, Melchizedek,
Meshezabel, Mephibosheth,
Nebuchadnezzer, Belshazzar—
whew! Please let me catch my breath!

Zephaniah, Zedekiah,
Zadok, and Zerubbabel—
pronouncing all these Bible names
gives me lots of troubable.

Jehoshaphat and Jozabad—
such complicated names!
Boy, I'm glad
my mom and dad
simply call me James.

Flaws

Moses was a drifter, Joseph was a dreamer,
Abraham would sometimes stretch the truth;
Sarah was a scoffer, Jacob was a schemer,
and even David could be quite uncouth.

These folks, they had their share of faults and foibles,
for all of them were obviously flawed,
but still in spite of all their traits and troubles,
somehow their lives were mightily used by God.

Sometimes I am a drifter, sometimes I am a dreamer,
and yes, sometimes I also stretch the truth;
sometimes I am a scoffer, sometimes I am a schemer,
and I confess, at times I'm quite uncouth.

But still in spite of all my
        flaws and failures,
and all the silly things
        I say and do,
like Moses, Joseph,
        Abraham, and Sarah,
I know my God can use me mightily too.

Multiple Choice

Choose one.
a. God is good.
b. God is love.
c. God is gracious.
d. All of the above.

Scripture Index

Genesis 1:1—2:4 16-17

Genesis 1:3-5 18

Genesis 1:6-8 19

Genesis 1:21 20

Genesis 1:27 25

Genesis 2:7 28, 30-31

Genesis 2:8-17 26

Genesis 2:18-20 34-35

Genesis 2:21-24 32

Genesis 3 36

Genesis 4 37

Genesis 5:27 38

Genesis 6:9-22 40-41

Genesis 6:14 56

Genesis 7 58-59

Genesis 7:1-3 42

Genesis 9:8-17 60-61

Genesis 11:1-9 63

Genesis 15:5 68-69

Genesis 18:10-15; 21:1-7
  70-71

Genesis 19:15-26 66

Genesis 22 72-73

Genesis 22:15-18 67

Genesis 24 74

Genesis 25:27-34 75

Genesis 32:22-32 78-79

Genesis 37:4 80

Genesis 37:6-9 82

Genesis 37:28 81

Genesis 45:1-15 83

Exodus 2:1-10 84-85

Exodus 4:10-17 86-87

Exodus 7—12 88-91

Exodus 8 92-93

Exodus 12:31-38 95

Exodus 14:15-22 96-97

Exodus 14:23-31 98-99

Exodus 15:20, 21 100-101

Exodus 16 102-103

Exodus 17:7 104

Exodus 20:1-17 105

Exodus 32 106-107

Exodus 32:19, 20 108-109

Numbers 16 110-11

Numbers 22 114

Joshua 6 116-17

Joshua 10 118

Judges 4 119

Judges 4:15-24 120

Judges 7 121

Judges 13—16 122-23

Judges 16:3 124

Judges 16:17-21 125

Ruth 1, 2 126-27

1 Samuel 3:11-14 128-29

1 Samuel 15:24-29 130

1 Samuel 16 132-33

1 Samuel 16:18 131

1 Samuel 17 134-35

1 Samuel 17:38, 39 136-37

1 Samuel 17:40-51 138-39

1 Samuel 17:44 140-41

1 Samuel 18:1-4; 20
  142-43

2 Samuel 6:12-23 144-45

2 Samuel 18 146-47

1 Kings 3 158

1 Kings 3, 4 156-57

1 Kings 11:2, 3 159

1 Kings 16:30-33 160

1 Kings 17:2-7 161

1 Kings 18 162-63

2 Kings 9 164

2 Kings 9:20 165

2 Chronicles 11:18-22
  166-67

2 Chronicles 20:20-30
  168-69

Esther 5:1-4; 7 171

Psalm 23 149

Psalm 42 150-51

Psalm 37:5 55

Psalm 86:12 152-53

Psalm 139 154-55

Ezekiel 37:1-14 182-83

Daniel 1:8-17 172-73

Daniel 3 174-75

Daniel 3:25, 28 176

Daniel 6 180-81

Daniel 6:19-22 178-79

Jonah 1, 2 184-85

Subject Index

Abraham 15, 67, 68-69,
    70-71, 72-73, 187
Absalom 146-47
Adam 28, 29, 30-31,
    32, 33, 34-35, 36
Babel 63, 64-65
Balaam's donkey 114, 177
Bible (general) 10-11,
    14, 15, 186
Cain and Abel 37
Creation 16-17, 18, 19,
    20, 21, 22-23, 24-25
Daniel 172-73, 178-79,
    180-81
David 131, 132-33,
    136-37, 138-39,
    142-43, 144-45,
    148, 177, 187
Deborah 15, 119
Elijah 160, 161, 162-63
Esau 75
Esther 15, 171
Eve 32, 33, 36
Exodus, the 95, 96-97
Ezekiel 182-83
Garden of Eden 26-27
Gideon 15, 122

God (general) 12-13, 106-
    107, 149, 187, 188-89
Goliath 134-35, 136-
    37, 138-39, 140-41
Isaac 70-71, 72-73, 74
Israelites 88-91, 95,
    98-99, 100-101,
    102-103, 106-107,
    112-13, 116-17, 168-
    69, 170, 171
Jacob 75, 76-77,
    78-79, 187
Jael 15, 120
Jehoshaphat 168-69
Jehu 165
Jezebel 164
Jonah 184-85
Jonathan 142-43
Joseph 15, 80, 81, 82,
    83, 187
Joshua 15, 115, 116-
    17, 118
Korah 110-11
Lot's wife 66
Methuselah 38
Miriam 100-101

Moses 15, 84-85, 86-
    87, 88-91, 96-97,
    98-99, 100-101, 104,
    105, 108-109, 110-11,
    112-13, 177, 187
Noah and the flood
    39, 40-41, 42, 43,
    44-45, 46-47, 48,
    49, 50-51, 52-53,
    54, 55, 56, 57,
    58-59, 60-61, 62
Plagues 88-91, 92-93,
    94
Rebekah 74
Rehoboam 166-67
Ruth 15, 126-27
Samson 122-23, 124, 125
Samuel 128-29, 132-33
Sarah 70-71, 187
Saul 130, 136-37
Shadrach, Meshach,
    and Abednego
    174-75, 176, 177
Solomon 156-57, 158, 159
Ten Commandments
    105, 108-109